# Monologues

## FOR

# Teenagers

### KARSHNER

Dramaline

Dramaline Publications
36-851 Palm View Road
Rancho Mirage, CA 92270
Phone 619/770-6076
Fax 619/770-4507

This book is printed on 55# Glatfelter acid-free paper. A paper that meets the requirements of the American Standard of Permanence of paper for printed library material.

# CONTENTS

# YOUNG WOMEN

# KATHRYN

*Kathryn, emotionally damaged by child molestation, recalls her father's indiscretions.*

It's hard. It's very hard to talk about. I mean . . . you know. It started when I was just six or seven years old. Just six or seven. He'd come into my room at night. I'd wake up and there he'd be. There he'd be, standing there. Standing there looking down at me, staring at me. He was always very quiet. I don't ever remember him saying anything. No, not a word. He'd, he'd sit down on the bed next to me and—he'd put his hand under the covers and start touching me. I don't know what I felt. I was confused. I mean, after all, he was my *father*. I thought it was all right, I guess. No! I don't know. Like I said, it was all so confusing.

As time went by, he got bolder and bolder and—he'd pull back the covers and stand me up and—and then he'd take off his clothes and make me touch him—do things to him. He'd take my hands and guide me. I was afraid to cry or not do what he wanted. I thought crying or not doing what he wanted would mean I was being bad. A child doesn't know. How can you know? With your *father*? You trust him and think it's all right, that it's normal. But then, at the same time, you know it isn't. I don't know. It's . . . it's hard to explain.

Now, thinking back, now it makes you sick inside and ashamed and you feel awful—guilty. You feel guilty and you didn't do anything wrong.

It's been years, but I still can't get it out of my mind. And it makes getting along with boys super hard. I mean, when they try to kiss me or touch me or anything, I go crazy.

I don't know what to do. I just don't know what to do.

*I don't pretend to be an ordinary housewife.*

—Elizabeth Taylor

# LINDA

*Linda refuses to do her brother's work.*

Hey, like c'mon! Gimme a break! I cleaned up yesterday. Did the toilets, did the mirrors, changed the sheets. Like when was the last time you changed sheets? (*Pause for response.*)

Yeah. Right. And you know why? 'Cause sheets are murder, that's why. Walking back and forth around king-size beds. I mean, like—forget it! (*Pause for response.*)

What? Are you kidding? Forget it! Go screw a gopher. Today—*you've* got it. I'm not taking two days in a row. It's your turn to clean up . . . jerk-off! (*Pause for response.*)

Hey, that's your problem. You can see her later. I'm not about to do your work so you'll have time to run around with Darlene. Remember the last time when I took two days in a row so you could mess around with Larry? You still owe me for that, lame-o. This time, no cop-outs. I'm outta here to the mall. Look at it this way—maybe doing dishes will get some of the dirt out from under your fingernails. (*Beat for response.*)

So? Call her up and tell her you're going to be late. What is it with the bitch, anyway? She can't wait a couple of hours? Jeez. And remember, don't stack without drying, okay? Leaving soap film on dishes can give you diarrhea. And, oh yeah, don't leave the trash cans in the driveway again, retardo. I gotta go. (*Pause for his complaint.*)

Tough. You're breaking my heart. Like I'm really going to worry about it, right? I'm really going to be sick to death over thinking of you here doing your job for a change. I'll be like real sick because of it. Sick to death. So sick I won't be able to eat more than three burgers, a side of crinkle fries, a couple of Classic Cokes, and a Snickers bar. See ya later, weirdo. (*She exits.*)

*When I saw my first screen test I ran from the projection room screaming.*

—Bette Davis (Ruth Elizabeth Davis)

# KIM

*Kim has just cracked up her father's new car and is sharing her anguish with her friend, Janet.*

(*Indicating the car.*) Just look at it! Can you believe it? Is that a mess? Is that trashed, or what? The whole side, Janet. Dad'll freak. He'll kill me for sure. (*Pause.*)

Of course I'm going to tell him. I've got to tell 'im. But *how?* That's the question. (*Pause.*)

No, it wasn't the other guy's fault. I wish it was. It was mine. I didn't see him and I ran right into him. I don't know where he came from. I was busy changing a tape at the time. I really clobbered him good. A shiny black Cadillac. I turned it into this big, wrinkled prune.

(*Pointing at her father's car.*) Wow! Check it out, Janet. You ever see such a crumpled up mess in your entire life? (*Pause for Janet's remark.*)

No, I'm okay, fine, not so much as a scratch. (*Pause.*) Whaddaya mean, lucky? If I was lucky I would have been killed. I'm dead meat anyway as soon as Dad sees this. (*Pause for Janet.*)

Just a scratch? Are you kidding? You know how much just a scratch costs to repair these days? A thousand bucks, at least. You're looking at big bucks here, Janet—elephant dollars! And they'll raise the insurance rates. My dad lives like in constant fear of that, of our insurance rates going up, you know. He's always ranting about it. He's got this thing about insurance. Damn! And the very first time I drive it, too.

Do me a favor, will you? Come on home with me. It'll be easier if you're there. I'll show it to Mom first. She'll be upset but not unreasonable like Dad and maybe she'll figure out a way of telling him without me getting murdered. Is your mother like that? (*Pause for Janet's answer.*)

Yeah, right, mine, too. She's really cool. Moms are neat when things get crazy.

*I want to go on until they have to shoot me.*
—Barbara Stanwyck (Ruby Stevens)

# MARY

*Mary bemoans the loss of her boyfriend.*

Tough? Are you kidding? It was a killer. I mean, like we'd been going together for a long time. Like steady, Ron and I.

I met him in English class. He was an "A" student, a brain. I was lame. He knew everything about that stuff. Like all about past participles and how to diagram sentences and that. He was one smart dude. And cute. Cute was better than the fact he could diagram stupid sentences. Hey, anybody can learn to diagram sentences, but you can't learn to be cute. Anyway, we started dating. At first, like going to movies on the weekends. Then we started going steady and we were together all the time. After school every day, every minute on weekends. For almost three years. We even talked about getting married.

Then this new girl moves here from Canada, okay? She was real slinky, with legs like toothpicks, and she spoke with this kind of accent that —between you and me—I think she put on, and all the guys flipped for her. I thought she was a big rodent nerd. Then Corky, Ron's best friend, he like dates her for a while and then they break up. Next thing is, Ron alluva sudden starts making these excuses why he can't see me so much, okay? He says his grades are falling off because of it. Hey!, is this bull, or what? Ron could memorize the phone book in half an hour.

Then he starts copping out on weekends. And when I'd call him, it was like he wasn't listening and I was talking into this empty phone, or something.Then Corky tells me that Ron's sneaking around with Carla. Carla, that was the skinny slut's name.

When I hit him with it, the turkey denied it and tried to lie out of it. But I didn't buy it. So one afternoon I showed up unexpected at Ron's house and caught him with his hand on Carla's boob.

I like really hurt for a while. And I still think about him too. A lot. I try not to, but—hey!

*This is for posterity. Everything
I do will be on film forever.*

—Barbra Streisand

# MINDY

*Mindy rambles in her effervescent, non-stop manner.*

I like dogs a lot but I like cats better because cats are quiet and take care of themselves and dogs dump on your rug and have to be trained and that because that's what I've always run into with dogs chewing up everything and making this mess and it's awful but I still don't hate them because I like all animals but cats are best and birds if they're not caged so they can fly and be free and that because it's terrible to cage up anything because how would you like to be locked up and trapped and not be able to mess around and stuff and be a person like animals can't be animals when they're caged up because it's not their real home like on this desert or in this jungle someplace so it's horrible not to be free like these people you see in pictures sometimes behind wire fences like animals and being kept there against their will without proper food and nutrition and they shrivel up and look like little reeds and have fear in their eyes and like you can't see something like that without thinking about how we've got it made and we shouldn't be so much into ourselves and so mellowed-out about the world and not care about the people and the animals and all of that instead of cute clothes and making out and pizza while here are all these burnt-out people without food or even TV and it's all too much of a downer to think about so I don't know why I brought it up when all I wanted to say was that cats are cool.

# MARCIE

*Marcie speaks of the importance of her room. It is her sanctuary, her haven, her special place.*

It's the very best place in the world. I go there whenever things get crazy. Like they seem to get a lot of the time. I go there and close the door and lock myself in with all my stuff and I feel safe and like nobody or anything can hurt me. It's my special place. A place where I can dream and hang out and think personal thoughts and be free.

If it wasn't for my room, I don't know what I'd do. Sometimes when I'm real sad, I go there and cry where nobody can see me and I can let it all out. It's a place where I'm happy, too. It's very important to have a place that's all yours; a place where it's like your own world, kind of; a place where you can be alone with the things that are important to you: your clothes, your magazines, your sounds, your phone, your pictures and stuff. And your special, secret stuff that nobody knows anything about but you. Sometimes I get into this fantasy thing in my room and create stories and situations in my mind. It's neat. It makes me feel good to make up things and dream and go far out mentally.

I think everybody needs a place where they can go and be alone and away from other people for a while and be private and do and think what they like. I think older people—my parents, for example, our world leaders for sure—should have a room, a special room of their own where they can get off by themselves. Maybe if they did, they wouldn't be so uptight all the time, so crazed, you know.

Every person in the world should have their private place where they can go and let down and be just plain "them" for a few minutes every day. I think it would help them get perspective. Everybody's so rushed and intense. It seems like nobody wants to be private anymore.

*The best way for me to prove myself as a person is to prove myself as an actress.*

—Marilyn Monroe
(Norma Jean Baker or Mortenson)

# LANA

*Lana is too hip and is not about to waste her life in her "totally sixties" hometown. In this speech, she talks of her rock--musician boyfriend, about joining him soon in Los Angeles.*

(*She has a letter.*) Hey, look! I got this letter. From Tom. It came yesterday. He's out in L.A. doing gigs. He says L.A.'s *happening.* Says it's where most of the heavy players are, the good jams. He enclosed this picture. Here, look. (*She shares the photograph with her friend.*)

Don't you just love his orange hair? What a touch. Tom's something else. He said he sat in in this place in the Valley the other night and that he blew them away. Listen to this: (*She reads from the letter.*) "This important dude from Capitol Records came by and really got off on my jams. Thought I was real heavy. Said he's going to try to get me some session work." He goes on. I gotta get myself out there, man. (*Beat for response.*)

How do you think? I'll hitch. (*Pause.*) C'mon, it's not that dangerous. Anyway, I can't take any chances with a cool dude like Tom out there with all those tight little units. Beach babes and Beverly Hills ladies.

My parents'll freak. They don't dig Tom. But I love him to the quantum. He's an ace dude and he's going to happen big. Bet on it. I'll get myself some money together or get Chinese-eyed trying, one or the other. And then—I'm outta here. I told Tom I was coming and it really amped him. Said I could rack out in this big house full of musicians in some place called Venice. Says it's real cool, fully munga. Even though I'm still a squid, I'm old enough to know what I want. I'm not about to go vegging out in this dork-ball, nowhere burg. Forget it. It's the pits. Totally sixties.

*I have no regrets. I wouldn't have lived my life the way I did if I was going to worry about what people were going to say.*

—Ingrid Bergman

# JULIE

*Julie experiences a quick emotional shift when she discovers that Kerry is amenable to her proposal not to go steady.*

Kerry, this is, a—like this is like kinda real hard for me to say, you know. But . . . but we've been going together steady now for almost five months, okay? (*Pause.*) How many? (*Pause.*)

Okay, four. Like I was saying—we've been going steady for almost four months and it's really neat and all that and you're a nice guy and I really like you a lot. Okay? (*Pause.*)

Yes, sure, I know you like me, too. I know that. But, let me finish. Like we've been seeing each other and nobody else all the time, okay? After school every day and every weekend and everything. We're always together. Always.

What I mean is . . . what I'm trying to say here is . . . is that maybe we're tying ourselves down too much at our age and that it really isn't fair for someone like you who is real cute and who would probably like to date a bunch of other girls to feel obligated to just one person, you know. And to be super honest, sometimes I'd like to be alone and be able to mess around with Jane and Esther and stuff.

What I'm trying to say is, is that maybe we should think about not going steady anymore. Now I know what you're going to say, okay? But don't get the idea that I'm trying to . . . (*She is interrupted by Kerry.*) What? (*Pause.*) You what? (*Pause.*) It's okay with you? Just like that, it's okay with you? I mean, I barely get it out of my mouth and it's all right with you. Wow! Ah ha! I get it! Kathryn Anderson, right?

(*Break for his response.*) Don't give me that. (*Pause.*) Oh yeah, sure, that's your story! Here I just kind of hint that maybe we shouldn't see each other so much and right away you want to break it off. (*Pause.*)

You do, too. You just said so. It's so easy for you. And after just three months, too! You've just been waiting for a chance to break it off so you can start dating that jerk Kathryn Anderson because her father owns a Chevy dealership. How do you think it makes me feel knowing that all the time we've been going together you've had the hots for someone else? (*Pause.*)

Oh no, huh uh. Don't go trying to smooth it over. I don't believe this! I don't . . . (*She is interrupted.*)

You do? No you don't. (*Pause.*) You do? No. (*Pause.*) No you don't, you're just saying that. Do you really? (*Pause.*) Honest? (*Pause.*) You really like me that much? No kidding, Kerry? (*Pause.*) Sure, of course I like you. You kidding? More than anything. You're the coolest guy in school. (*Pause.*)

Break up? Who said anything about breaking up? All I was saying is that maybe you felt tied down, that's all. I was just giving you a way out, okay? Hey! I mean, gee whiz, I was just thinking of you, that's all, you know. (*Pause.*)

Sure I want to keep going steady. You kidding? (*Pause.*) You do? (*Pause.*) Me too.

(*Reaction.*) There's the bell! I'll meet you out front like always, okay? And about Kathy Anderson . . . my dad says everything her father owns is on paper.

*You can't get spoiled if you do your own ironing.*

—Meryl Streep

# LOUISE

*Louise, a teenage prostitute, a product of parental indifference, is hardened to the Mean Streets.*

I just couldn't take Oakdale anymore. It was a nothing town with nothing happening. Men out of work, women bored and desperate. It was a burned-out city with no future. A regular modern tragedy.

I was a poor student. Didn't go much for the books. Didn't cut it with my teachers. And my parents we're more or less indifferent. If things would have been better at home, maybe I would have tried to hang in. But Dad was always out of work, it seemed, and hanging around the house depressed and drunk and ugly. I tried to get something going with him lots of times, but he treated me like I wasn't there. And Mom didn't have much to say about anything. She didn't seem to give a damn. It was like life had passed her by, ya know? She had this zero attitude—a zombie. Pitiful. Anyway, they never gave me any support and I was bummed out being in the middle of their mess. So I came to the city because I had this promise of a job from this guy I met who was passing through Oakdale selling solar junk. He said to look him up and he'd get me straight.

He didn't get me anything. All he wanted was to make it with me. We lived together for a while and I got a job at Macy's in the notions department. Most of the time I was broke and my thing with Ron, the solar guy, was a real downer.

I got kind of thick with this girl down the hall from us, Rose, and she asked me if I wanted to make some real money. She introduced me to Leon. He was a pimp and was very smooth and convincing. So I started turning tricks. Young girls are always in big demand.

That was eighteen months ago. Today I'm doing about three Johns a day and I'm making decent bread. And I'm living in a decent place on Riverside Drive. It's a wild life, but you get used to it after a while. Most Johns are cool. Some are strange and want to get into odd trips, which I don't do. You learn to read each situation and sense when there's danger. There's all kinds of weird people out there, let me tell you.

My dad split from home and I've been sending money back to Mom. She thinks I'm in computers. If she knew what I was doing she'd, she'd . . . I hate to think about it. But I look on it as a job, nothing more. There's no feeling connected with any of it. It's a cold business. You make a date, you do it, you get paid, you get out. Nobody gets hurt. Maybe.

---

*I've had a fascinating life. I don't think I'm the least bit peculiar, but people tell me I am.*

—Katharine Hepburn

# JENNY

*Jenny speaks affectionately of a friend and neighbor.*

She lived in the next block. A couple of times a day she used to walk her little dog past the house. A terrier. She'd had a stroke, which had left her partially paralyzed on one side. She walked very slowly and it took her forever go make it 'round the block. I used to see her and talk with her almost every day. We'd talk about all kinds of things. She was a nice lady and always seemed intensely interested in me and what I had to say. Her name was Mrs. Jamison. Her son lived in Cincinnati and used to come see her once a month. She talked about him a lot, and you could tell she loved him and was super proud of him.

Last week, on the way home from school, I saw the emergency van outside her place and I knew something was wrong. They took her to St. Joseph's hospital, and I visited her there two days later. She'd had another stroke and had fallen through a sliding-glass door and had lain naked all night before the guy who delivers bottled water discovered her the next morning. Her son was there and he was extremely nice. He told me how much his mother looked forward to talking with me and he thanked me for caring and coming to visit.

Mrs. Jamison looked pretty in a pink nightgown. I told her I was taking care of Muffy—her terrier—and this seemed to please her. We talked for a long time and she told me about her life as a young girl growing up in a rural area and how she used to walk two miles to school. Tears came to her eyes when she recalled old times at home with her brothers and sisters. It was a wonderful visit. Sweet. Sweet, but also sad.

She died yesterday. Her son came over and told us. And he told me that Mrs. Jamison wanted me to have Muffy.

I miss her. The neighborhood has a hole in it that she used to fill. And I think about her a lot. I learned from her. I learned that when you're old and alone, life is something you have to face bravely. It takes courage to face it day after day and not complain. And she never did. She was always smiling.

*I used to tremble from nerves so badly that the only way I could hold my head steady was to lower my chin practically to my chest and look up at Bogie. That was the beginning of The Look.*

—Lauren Bacall (Betty Jean Peske)

# DIANE

*Diane confesses that all the erudition in the world cannot replace human interaction.*

Oh, Roger's friendly enough, all right, but I don't think it means anything. He's nice because he wants to copy my homework, that's all. He comes into English class early and copies my notes almost every day. If he wasn't so darned cute, I'd tell him to go iron a prune. I know I'm being used, I know that. But, who knows, maybe someday he'll ask me out.

Being smart is all right, but it can also have its drawbacks because often your knowledge intimidates people. Especially boys. Although Roger appears to be intelligent. And he's very funny. He cracks me up. But I don't think he cares if I live or die. Most guys are indifferent to girls like me. You know—plain, serious, on the Honor Roll. On the Honor Roll can be this big negative because right away people prejudge you as an intellectual; and intellectual means dud. And, to be perfectly honest, most people on the Honor Roll *are* pretty strange.

I know I'm super shy. I've always known that. That's the reason I got into books. I found escape in them. It was a way of insulating myself. I've always been self-conscious and I have trouble making small talk. Especially with boys. Around them I'm invariably tongue-tied and frightened. I come apart. I kind of like panic. It's always a very traumatic experience, and it makes me actually hurt inside. It's terrible feeling awkward and afraid.

With books, on the other hand, I'm totally comfortable. They're dispassionate and I control *them*. And I do get a lot of pleasure from them. But when you're living in books, you're living second-hand.They're neat, but definitely second-hand.

People who can be easy with others have it made. I'm a much richer person because of my books and my studies, I'm sure of it. But sometimes . . . sometimes I feel poor in the heart.

*Films are much more my level.*
*On stage I never felt quite enough.*

—Julie Andrews (Julia Wells)

# MARTHA

*Martha describes her day as a truant.*

I ditched school with Alice last Wednesday. We went to the mall. It's weird during the week like that and not as neat as on Saturdays when all your friends are messing around there, too. It's real quiet and kind of spacey and not crowded and you feel strange being the only teenagers in the whole place. And I felt like people were staring at me because I'd cut school. It's like everybody in the place knew it, you know. I felt great-big and conspicuous and totally guilty. Like this creep, or a criminal, or something, you know. But not Alice. She ditches all the time. At least three times a month. To her it's nothing.

We pigged out on munchies and watched people. Mostly housewives. Most of them with little kids. And most of them were fat and out-of-shape. I guess that's what happens when you get married and have babies. It was kind of depressing. This one woman was huge and fat and was wearing activewear and she really grossed me out. Her butt was huge and real lumpy like bread dough and it moved around in her sweats like Jell-O inside a balloon. I kept imagining her nude and the thought nearly made me barf.

We went to Penney's and looked at the cosmetics and spritzed ourselves with cologne. Then we went to the clothing department and tried on a bunch of stuff. Alice knew the names of all the salespeople because of going there all the time on her ditch days. I got the feeling they didn't appreciate us rooting through the racks and mixing up the sizes.

Then we go up to the furniture department and test mattresses and pretend we're in this adult motel with David Carpenter and Harvey Melnick. Then we left at three o'clock because that's when school lets out, so we had to go home and act normal and complain about homework.

Next week Alice wants me to ditch with her again and go check out the auto show. She says they hand out all kinds of neat freebies like yardsticks and balloons and brochures and stuff. Okay, I guess, if you're into yardsticks and balloons.

I don't know. I'm not sure. I'll have to think about ditching again. Because I think maybe the guilt's worse than going to school.

---

*I had the stage mother of all time. If I wasn't well, and didn't go on, she'd yell,* "Get out on that stage or I'll tie you to the bedpost."

—Judy Garland (Frances Gumm)

# FRANCES

*Frances is pregnant. Here she expresses her feelings of frustration, anger, and fear.*

He'd never go for it. Marriage? Are you kidding? Just wait till he finds out. He'll freak for sure. He'll probably hate me. Blame me for it. As if he didn't have anything to do with it. I kept telling him to use something, but no. . . . I guess I can't put all the blame on Don, though. It takes two. Besides, who needs marriage, anyway? Me? No way. Hey, gimme a break. Married with a kid at my age? Sitting around some crummy apartment all day watching sitcom reruns? Marriage is out.

You know, getting pregnant's like you're being punished for having sex. It's kind of like nature's way of getting even, you know. Being a woman's hell, Shirley. We get the bad end of it. Get stuck with this complicated body. Guys, they've really got it made. It must really be neat being a guy, you know. No monthly uglies. No getting pregnant. No childbirth. Being a woman is a *mess.*

I still can't believe it. I just can't. Pregnant! You think it'll never happen to you. You get away with it and you get away with it and you keep taking chances because you think you're immune. You think you're different. You think you're cool. Then you go over a few days. At first you figure it's because you had the flu, or something. You make up stories, justify. Then you miss a whole month and you go crazy. After I saw the doctor, I still couldn't believe it. I told myself, "This can't be happening to me." But then you realize that it is, that it all isn't just some crazy nightmare. And then you get sick inside and feel trapped and hate yourself and life and everything. You feel desperate and awful. Like I feel right now.

I thought I was so cool. I thought I was so wise. I thought I knew everything. Alice, what am I going to do?

*Everybody imitated my fuller mouth, my darker eyebrows. But I wouldn't copy anybody. If I can't be me, I don't want to be anybody. I was born that way.*

—Joan Crawford
(Lucille Lesueur, known for a time as Billie Cassin)

# CINDY

*Cindy tells of her parents' split, speaking insightfully regarding the destructiveness of emotional dishonesty.*

Mom and Dad split up last December. Right before the holidays. You'd think they could have at least waited till after.

I felt it coming. They'd been going at each other for a long time. Arguing, constantly bickering. And it kept getting worse. It was awful. Sometimes I could hear them shouting at each other all the way upstairs. It's terrible hearing people say hurtful things to each other. And when it's your parents. . . .

I wonder how long they'd felt this way about each other? Felt this kind of resentment, I mean? It couldn't have always been like that. I suppose it's just something that happens, I guess. Too bad.

I've given it a lot of thought. I think these things happen because people let things build up over the years, not say what's on their minds. I mean, like things that are bugging them, you know. I know with Harry Applebaum and me it was like that. We started out liking each other a lot, but after a while, little by little, it got to be this trap for me, and I didn't know how to tell him how I felt without hurting his feelings, so I didn't say anything. But inside I was going crazy and feeling like this prisoner. My bars were all these feelings I never let out that were pressing in around me. Does that make sense? Until it got so I really resented him. Not for him, but because of me. Because of me not being me. So I started being mean to him intentionally in these strange little ways until I forced this tremendous screaming argument, and it was over. It was a relief not being tied down anymore, but it didn't have to end that way, on like this bad note, you know.

I think what it all boils down to is honesty. I mean, being straight about what you're feeling. It seems so much easier to just avoid stuff. But when you do, you don't ever really get rid of it. Ever. You just push it down inside, where it turns rotten and ruins you and your relationships.

With Harry and me it was only six months. But with Mom and Dad it was twenty years. *Twenty years.* Just think of what twenty years of dishonesty has to do to people. After all that time—it all comes out like bullets.

---

*I never said, "I want to be alone."*
*I only said, "I want to be let alone."*

—Greta Garbo (Greta Gustafson)

# YOUNG MEN

# KEN

*Ken is determined to go his own way, not to tread the traditional family path. He eschews Yale in favor of a business education, perhaps a future in marketing.*

Hey, Joe, c'mon! To be real up-front, I don't really give a crap what you think, okay? I'm not about to go to Yale and that's that! (*Pause for response.*)

Right. I don't intend to go along with something just because it's expected, just because Dad and our grandfather and great-grandfather did it. I'm not following in footprints. I'm making my own, okay? (*Pause.*)

Responsible? Responsible to whom? I'm only responsible for me! For *me,* understand? Not for the family and Dad and Uncle Otis or the Brookmyers or the Gallaghers or anybody else. Yale. Big damned deal! Hell, Joe, you don't want to go there any more than I do. Be honest. But you will. You'll sell out because of what it means and how it'll look and because you're part of the package. (*Pause.*)

C'mon. Bullshit! You're going because it's safe and you'll get your law degree and move into the firm and hang out at the club and play like a liberal. Not me. Besides, I couldn't make the requirements anyhow. I'd bomb for sure. A nice little liberal arts college somewhere suits me fine—me and my I.Q. Hell, I'd freak at Yale pretending I was smart. Nope, Yale's out. Even if it means pissing Dad off. Besides, I kinda think I'd like to get into retail. (*Pause.*)

Yeah, retail. Christ, you act like I just said a dirty word, or something. I'm going to say it again, so you'd better cover up your delicate little ears—*retail*! Joe, whether you know it or not, there are actually people out there selling things to other people. I know it's hard for someone like you to grasp, but there are such individuals. In fact, I even spoke to a Kmart manager the other day. Walked right up to him and said, "Pardon me, where's the stationery section?" And you know what? The man actually understood English. And, hey, he was wearing shoes. Why, he probably hadn't bitten the head off a chicken in a week.

Sorry to break the pattern, Joe, but Yale's out. You go. Buy suits. Get ties. Polish up your blazer buttons. You'll love it, it's you. As for me? Look for me in Penney's window.

---

*Once you're a star actor, people start asking you questions about politics, astronomy, and birth control.*

—Marlon Brando

# DOUG

*Doug comes down hard on the films of yesteryear.*

My mom and dad and their friends are always raving about how great the old movies were. About how they had less sex and violence, how they were more romantic, how much better the actors were. No way.

I've watched some of these old flicks. A lot of them. A waste, man, a total waste. Like *Gone With The Wind,* my mom's favorite. There's no violence in that? The *Civil War*? Like there's this one scene where this whole town's on fire and people are screaming and there's blood and bodies all the way to Biloxi. And it's a heck of a lot more gruesome than movies today. Because it's this lyrical, contrived violence, which is a lot more horrible. And how about the acting? Wow! Awful! Like in this one scene where Scarlett's up on this hill doing this big dramatic number and gesturing all over the place like some crazed freak. Hey, we've got girls in our drama class who can do better acting than that.

Then there's this gangster movie with James Cagney, *White Heat*, where he goes and shoves this guy into the trunk of a car and slams the lid and then pumps bullets into it, wastes this dude with this crap-eating grin on his face. That's not *violent?* Hey, like do me a favor. When I mention it to my dad, he says it's not as bad as today because you never see the guy get it. Hey, that's worse. Apparently he's never heard of imagination. Like the old movies with the girl chained to this log going into this gigantic buzzsaw. Is that ever gross, or what? You can just imagine her being chewed up like a big fat orange in a garbage disposal. And the sex. Hey, sometime scope out the babes in a Busby Berkeley movie.

They're right about one thing, though. They don't make 'em like the used to. And boy—are we ever lucky.

---

*Do I subscribe to the Olivier school of acting?*
*Ah, nuts. I'm an actor. I just do what comes naturally.*

—Humphrey Bogart

# MIKE

*Mike tells of a recent brush with prostitution.*

We drove up on Saturday night. To this place that is about fifteen miles the other side of the county line. Like in the middle
of nowhere, okay? It was this old, dilapidated farmhouse off
the main road. Like set way back, you know. And all you can
see is this little red light on the front porch. So we drive down
this lane and there are two or three other cars parked outside.

We all get out and go up to the front door and hit the bell
and this big dude comes and looks us up and down like we're
cops or something and wants to know how old we are. Brian
whips out his older brother's ID and shows it to the dude and
tells him we're all the same age and he lets us in. Inside, it's
like this big creepy Charles Addams kind of place, and it has
this bad, musty smell, like wet newspaper. The dude leads us
into this big front room, and there are about five women there
all made up real sexy and wearing these gowns that let you see
their boobs. Melons, babe, melons. Then the dude asks if we've
got money and tells us that it's a hundred bucks a pop. A
hundred bucks! Hey, maybe that was all we had between us,
okay? So what we do is pool our dough and it's decided that
I'm the guy because it was my idea and I'm the oldest, right?
Okay. So I go over and pick out this big blonde and she leads
me upstairs into a dimly lit room with nothing in it but a bed
and a chair. A bathroom is off. She goes in the bathroom and

comes out naked except for high-heeled shoes and comes over and begins to like start groping me, you know. Weird, man, weird. So like I make this excuse that I have to go to the bathroom, okay? I go in and lock the door and pull the lid down on the john and sit and think. I look around. The place stinks. I feel cheap. The whole thing is outrageous and sick. So what I do is climb up on a radiator and open this little window and squeeze out and drop down on this porch roof and then drop to the ground and beat it back to the car. The guys razz me like crazy. But what the hell? They had no idea what a bad scene it was, and how the whole thing made me sick. Then, I give them back their money and we all have this big laugh. On the way home, we stopped off at Wendy's and burgered out.

*If you got it, flaunt it.*

—Mel Brooks (Melvin Kaminsky)

# DONNY

*Donny tells of his battle with alcohol.*

I started in drinking when I was just fifteen. At this club—the
Bamboo Room, where I was playing bass with the Elements—
the name of this group. The keyboard guy, Eddie, who was
eighteen, he turned me on to beer. During a break, we went
across the street to this bar and Eddie ordered beers for me and
I drank them on the sly, ya know? I had two and I remember
that I really didn't like it all that much. And then after, when
we got out in the street, I felt dizzy and I thought something
was wrong with me for sure because things looked weird.
Eddie said it was the effects of the beer. I was kinda drunk.
That was the first time. But then, during the time we played at
the Bamboo Room, we'd go over and get beers during inter-
missions all the time. That started it.

I began to drink more and more and I moved up to vodka
and grapefruit juice—salty dogs. They had more kick, it
seemed, got me high in a hurry. Then, after a while, I'd drink
anything, no matter what. Gin, rum, wine—you name it, man.
Anything that would get me smashed because I dug being
behind booze. Then I started drinking before I went to school
in the mornings. Lots of times I didn't even remember being in
class. Sometimes for whole days I was messed up. Whole days,
man. It was a blast. I thought so at the time, anyway.

As time went by, it got so I couldn't be without the stuff. I was hooked. I was an alcoholic. Dependent. And I wasn't eating right and I was losing weight and looking beat. And I was getting these real bad stomach cramps and vomiting. I was in deep trouble, I knew that, but I couldn't come out of it. When my old man found out, he flipped. No sympathy, just a bunch of screaming and slapping me around, ya know? It was a bad scene. My folks were divorced, and like there was no family or anything, so I was just out there alone, bouncing off walls. My life was screwed.

Then it happened. Eddie, the keyboard man, he up and died, just like that. Hit the wall. Eighteen and *dead*. Doing blow, doing crack, doing—you name it—everything. Dead, man. Well, let me tell you, that really pulled me back, got me to thinking. So I asked for help and found it in AA. They're neat people, caring and supportive. It was a struggle, but I beat it. But I'll always have the problem. And I'm just a kid, too— just a kid.

---

*I don't want to achieve immortality through my work. I want to achieve it through not dying.*

—Woody Allen (Allen Stewart Koingsberg)

# JEFF

*Jeff expresses his sense of loss for his father.*

I don't think I ever really knew my father. Not really. I mean, not where it counts, that is, down deep. It always seemed like there was this distance between us, you know.

He was always so busy all of the time. And all I can remember about him when I was little was that he always seemed to either be coming or going. He was like this roomer who lived with us and ate with us and slept upstairs. We never spent much time together, just the two of us. And when we were together, like there was nothing happening, ya know? Seemed like nobody ever had time. Or made time. Or cared, maybe, I guess. I don't know. But I sure know how I feel now, now that he's dead. I really miss him a lot. And I wish he was still around so we could sit down and share things. And talk about things we never got into when he was alive. I mean, *real* things. Things from in here. (*He pounds his fist to his chest.*)

I've got all this love inside for him that never got out. Damn. Why didn't I ever tell him how I felt? Why? Why didn't I open up? Why is it so hard to get stuff out in the open? I mean like, love. Why is it so scary? (*He pauses, then looks up and addresses his remarks heavenward.*)

I love you Dad. I love you more than anything. And I'm sorry I never told you so, and that you never ever told me. I wish you were here so I could put my arms around you and hold you tight and tell you all the things I always wanted to say but never did. Like how much I respected you and how I thought you were a really neat guy and best father in the whole world and how you were something special. And I'd tell ya I love ya.

I love ya, Dad. I *love* ya!

*I was a fourteen-year-old boy for thirty years.*

—Mickey Rooney (Joe Yule, Jr.)

# DAVID

*Otis has acne and David is attempting to lift him from his doldrums by applying logic. Sort of.*

C'mon, Otis. You've gone and let this thing turn you around. Just look at you, you big turkey. I mean like what's the big deal here, anyway? So you've got a bad complexion. So what? So what else is new? More than half the guys in school have faces like frozen oatmeal. It's no big thing. It's your age. Our age. It's part of the teenage deal. It's got to do with growing up and getting whiskers and having strange dreams and that. You're no different than a zillion other guys your age. It's a worldwide thing. Young guys all over the planet have got bad skin. It's like this all-over problem, you know. And you know why? Because they're vending crap food everywhere now. You can buy a Big Mac and fries in any country. Even in Russia. Hey! Nobody's safe. 'Cause wherever there's grease, there's zits.

(*Pointing to his face.*) Look here. See this? What do you think this is? A zit, man. Like a big yellow headlight. They come. They go. They start out a little pimple, develop into ugly red bumps and wind up egg yolks. What can you do? Nothing. Ya can't fight nature. Hey, even Jack Archer has 'em. (*Pause.*)

You haven't noticed? Well, next time check it out. He covers 'em up with Erase and powder and stuff. But up close his face looks like the Alps.

So don't sit around bitching and moaning. Go get some Oxy Clean Pads, or something, okay? Or go see your friendly dermatologist, pinch—whatever. But do me and yourself a big favor—quit acting like a spaz. Do you know what? Know what, Otis? Your negative attitude lately is a whole lot more revolting than your complexion.

C'mon, let's get outta here and go on down to Smith's Dairy Store and suck up a hot fudge.

*My acting technique is to look up at God just before the camera rolls and say, "Give me a break."*

—James Caan

# LES

*Les tells of the rigors of his warehouse job.*

It was too much. Another month in that place and I'da been a broken person. Look, I may not be super swift, but I sure figured out in a hurry that lifting slabs of wallboard for a living isn't the way to conquer the world. Understand?

The other kid who worked there had been there for over four years and he actually liked the job. He dug the living shit out of lifting junk and assembling unfinished furniture. This guy could throw a vanity together in ten minutes. Some kind of stupid company record, or something. Big deal. Four years for that? Can you imagine? Some slobs never wise up. But not for me, man, no way. All that heavy lifting? Hey!, you wind up with a gigantic hernia, fast. Have 'em hanging down to your knees and swinging like bell clappers before you're twenty. Forget it. And get this: they used to back up this semi twice a month, loaded with refrigerators and ranges and washers and dryers and stuff, and we, the two of us, had to unload it. Two guys! Can you believe it?

(*Displaying his thumb, which is swathed in a bandage.*) See this thumb? Smashed between a food freezer and a brick wall. Neat, huh? This here is the kind of stuff that happens to you when you're an ape for a living. You get yourself bruised and battered and get ingrown toenails from wearing steel-tipped shoes eight hours a day.

(*Displaying his hands.*) You get permanent half-moons of grime where your cuticles used to be. Look!

The stock room—that's where we worked—it was up on the top floor. And it wasn't air conditioned because the executive creeps wouldn't spring for AC, so we sweated like pigs up there and lived on salt tablets. One day I pass out and go an' fall face-first into a crate of VCRs. The whole thing was insane, believe me. And for small bucks. Bird money. And you had to punch a time clock and if you got back from lunch even a minute late, they'd dock your ass. Can you blame me for quitting? The whole thing was really bizarre. For that kind of work—later.

> *There is a mixture of anarchy*
> *and discipline in the way I work.*
>
> —Robert De Niro

# COLIN

*Colin, a new kid on the scene, agonizes over his loneliness, his inability to relate. He speaks of the problems of readjustment, the cruel indifference of others.*

Meeting people, making new friends isn't easy. Not for me, anyhow. It never has been. It's tough. I've never been like this outgoing person who can just walk up to someone and start in talking just like that. Some kids can. I'm envious of them. They're lucky.

Coming here cold from Detroit and moving into this new neighborhood and starting a new school is murder. It's hard to settle in and readjust. It's like I'm alluva sudden from outer space here or something. Some kind of freak, you know. It seems like nobody wants to have anything to do with me. Back home, kids were friendly. Here—cold.

Unless you've been through it, you've got no idea how hard it is for a kid to make a change from one city to another. It's a killer. Here you are one day in comfortable surroundings and then, the next, alluva sudden you wake up in the middle of a damned jungle with everything foreign and strange. With no friends. That's the worst part of it. No friends.

I've discussed it with my parents, but they don't seem to understand. They expect you to just pick up and keep on going as usual. Easy for them, maybe, because they're working on an adult level where there's a lot more diplomacy. What they don't understand is that kids usually say what's on their minds.

And sometimes what's on their minds is that they think you're a nerd. So they'll say so and laugh and then other kids'll pick up on it and laugh, too, and then everyone thinks you're a nerd without even knowing anything about you.

You'd like to say, "Hey, creeps, give me a break." But you don't because you don't want to alienate them, you want to be accepted. So you take their crap and pretend it doesn't hurt. But it does. It does, and it makes you wonder why some people go out of their way to be such assholes.

*A lot of what acting is, is paying attention.*

—Robert Redford

# DENNIS

*Dennis finds the cost of dating intolerable, the entertainment lame, his expectations for a "good time" shattered.*

Hey, you got off cheap. My date cost me almost thirty bucks. (*Pause.*)

The hell it didn't! Look—with the movie, the pizza and stuff afterward—almost thirty. Thirty bucks! Way too heavy for me, man. Way outta my league, babe. Crazy. Like I'm this millionaire here, or something?

Hey, I say let *them* kick in once in a while, okay? Who made up this rule that says the guy's gotta always handle it? Thirty bucks. *Thirty lousy bucks!* And the flick was real trash. Another Hollywood rip-off. What do those jerks think's going on out here, anyway? Like we're this bunch of cornball farmers here, or something? It was same old cop, car crash, blow-'em-away movie bullshit.

(*He points his finger like a gun.*) *Freeze!* You know what? Hollywood would be in deep creative trouble without the word "freeze," man. Airheads! And I didn't even make out, either. She gave me all this stuff about how she had to get to know me better and all that. She kidding? How come she didn't have to get to know half the basketball team better? How 'bout that, huh? I should have borrowed your letter sweater. I'da worn that, she'd been in my pants faster than a tailor.

But the bucks, man, that's the killer. *Thirty dollars!* How do they expect kids to handle these kind of prices? A buck seventy-five for a watery Coke, three bucks for stale popcorn. Then she goes and gets the hots for a Mounds bar.

(*He mimics a girl's voice.*) "Could I have a Mounds bar, Dennis?" There goes another two bucks down the tubes so she can get a bunch of coconut in her braces.

No more expensive dates. Next time I take her down to the Chevron station and we watch 'em wax a Buick.

---

*The exciting thing about making movies today is that everything is up for grabs. And you had better grab.*

—Michael Douglas

# JOHN

*John, frustrated, tells of his family's rejection of the idea of him driving.*

It isn't like I've never been behind the wheel before, ya know? I've had my permit for over six months. You know what it is, Steve? Parents just can't admit that you're growing up, that's what.

You should have heard 'em last night. A couple of real geeks. They went nuts. Just because I want my own wheels. They wouldn't listen to reason; they were out of it. They hit me with all these negative statistics about teen drivers and the cost of insurance and how if I totaled the car and killed this entire family my dad would get the pants sued off him and lose his printing business. And my mom got super crazy dramatic and started in screaming about how she could visualize me going face-first through a windshield.

There was no reasoning with them. They were hysterical. What do they expect me to do? Ride buses for the rest of my life? Already I can see myself an old man getting from one side of the city to the other with transfers. What the hell is it with these people, Steve? Can't they remember when they were young?

And, oh yeah, how about this one? They don't mind if I take the car just so long as they're along. Can you believe this? Huh? Let me ask you, is this bizarre here, or what? Are you listening to me here?

How about being on a date and here you've got the old man and the old woman in the back seat? Is this a bizarre thought, or what? I mean, like here you are with your mom and dad in the back seat watching you and the babe and the speedometer like hawks and eating their homemade popcorn and making stupid comments like, "Watch the road, sonny." Man, I'm finished, my life is hist.

God, I'll never be free.

*My involvement goes deeper than acting or directing. I love every aspect of the creation of motion pictures and I guess I'm committed to it for life.*

—Clint Eastwood

# LARRY

*Larry speaks of his father's passing, expressing his sense of loss and abandonment.*

It was two years ago today that my dad died. Yep, already two years. And, you know, it's still hard to believe. I still look for him to come walking in the back door every night with this big grin on his face.

He died unexpectedly. I mean, like he was always so healthy and strong. He seemed like indestructible, you know. I don't remember him ever being sick a day. Then one night he comes home complaining of this pain, this burning sensation in his chest. Like, right here. . . . (*He presses a spot near the base of his sternum.*)

At first he thought it was the stomach flu or heartburn, or something. So he got a whole bunch of stuff from the drugstore and started watching his diet. But the pain didn't go away. In fact, it kept getting worse, to the point where one morning he couldn't go to work.

He finally broke down and went to the family doctor, who sent him to this specialist who said he had to have an operation because of this dark spot that showed up in the x-rays.

The night before he went to the hospital was the first time I ever remember seeing him afraid. The fear was in his eyes; you could see it. We all sat up real late that night because he didn't want to go to bed. The poor guy. He must have suspected something.

When they operated, they found that cancer was eating him alive and they told us he had maybe six months. It was a terrible thing. I remember how sick I got inside.

Mom decided to close up the house and rent us a place in Florida so Dad could be someplace warm and sunny till. . . . Then, unexpectedly, he died three days later. Just like that.

It really shook me up a lot and it took me a long time to get over it. The shock of it nailed me down for a while, you know. But I got over it, I mean the grieving part, that is. You have to. After a while, you have to let go. But I still think of him and I still miss him. It just isn't the same without him around. Like there's this place inside me that's empty, you know—a place he filled. I really miss him. A lot. And I always will, I guess. Hey, I mean, after all—he was my dad.

> *Once in a man's life, for one mortal moment, he must make a grab for immortality. If not, he has not lived.*
>
> —Sylvester Stallone

# DINO

*Frank, Mr. Everything, has committed suicide. This is difficult for Dino to comprehend. But introspection leads to revelations regarding the act.*

The last time I saw Frank was in the gym. He looked great. I mean, who would have thought that a guy like that, this buff dude, this super athlete who was super-smart, an honor student and everything, would kill himself? He had it all happening for him. But you never know, I guess, never know what's really going on inside a person. Like Frank. Here he must have had all these problems and nobody ever knew because he never let on. He always seemed to have it all together. He seemed like the last guy who would. . . .

When they told me, it blew me away. Like here he was, one minute this great-looking dude with ladies all over the place and then, the next minute—dead. Boom! Just like that. It sure makes you think. Makes you think a lot. About how many people are like this; about how many unhappy and messed up people are right on the edge, you know. I guess maybe in Frank's case he had lots of pressures. I understand his dad expected him to be the best at everything he did. Ralphie told me that one time he saw his old man slap him around because he got a "C" on his card. It must be a real bitch living up to someone else's expectations.

This is the third kid who's killed himself since I've been in this school. And it's hard to figure. I mean, with them being so young and all. I can understand if it's someone old or sick, or something. But when you've got your whole life ahead of you? Maybe life comes down on these kids real hard in some way and pushes them and gets them turned around and they don't know which way to go. And then drugs, they come into it a lot. Two of the kids were users, I know that for a fact. With them, at least you can kind of understand it, you know. Looking back, you can remember them sitting around spaced like their minds had hit a dead end. But Frank? This was a surprise. This was different. Poor dude. If he'd just opened up, let off some steam. Maybe that would have saved him. I wish I'd known him better. Maybe we could have talked. Maybe I could have helped him. Poor guy. If he'd just been able to ask for help. Damn.

*Acting is a question of absorbing other people's personalities and some of your own experience.*

—Paul Newman

# RALPH

*A disgruntled Ralph describes the lengths to which parents will go to disrupt his sack time.*

Saturdays I try to sleep, in but my mom's always banging around and everything. It never fails. Like doing the laundry and running the sweeper real loud and making all kinds of noise. It's like a war out there. Just on weekends. The rest of the week she's real quiet. I figure it's this plan to wake you up because they know you're real beat and want to sleep. It really kills them to see a kid comfortable. It's like this with a lot of stuff with parents. They go out of their way to mess up things you like to do. Although they always say not. But it's real easy to figure. I mean, hey!, face it, they just love to go out of their way to trash your fun. I think it's their way of getting even for not being young anymore. They forget what it was like when they were teens.

Adults—how do you figure them? I guess they don't have any fun or freedom anymore, so they don't want anyone else to have any either. Human nature. But it sure is a bitch and it really pisses you off sometimes. Like last weekend. Sunday. Alluva sudden my dad gets this wild hair about the screens, okay? After twelve years he figures out that the screens are dirty? C'mon. What happened was, he woke up early for a change and thought about me lying in bed sound asleep and warm and comfortable and the thought of it drove him bananas. So around seven o'clock—*seven o'clock!*—I hear this banging outside my window and I jump up because I think maybe somebody's trying to break into the house, or something. When I look out my window, I see my old man up on a ladder messing with my screen. I say, "You up already?" Most of the time he sleeps in till at least eleven. And he says, "I've been up for hours. Somebody's got to take care of these things around here." He said it with this real fake, weak voice. The kind they use when they're trying to make you feel guilty. I said, "Yeah." Then I went back to bed and sacked out till noon.

*I don't act, I react.*

—James Stewart

# STAN

*Stan rails against the military, the politicians, the dogs of war.*

Like some of these guys really get off on war, you know. I mean, they really dig the living shit out of blowing people away. They sit on their butts and figure out how to use all this high-tech military hardware we're building like crazy. Military jerks the world over are into war games, into checking out maps and getting involved in exercises. "Exercises." Exercises with bombs and boats and armies and missiles. Exercises in annihilation! We're talking blood alley here, buddy. We're talking bones and eyeballs and guts and guys lying around with their entrails oozing out on some God-forsaken beach someplace where five years later they'll be building a Sheraton hotel. Yeah, after a few years it's all forgotten like it never happened.

Our leaders, the leaders of these countries, lack enlightenment. They'll wind up destroying us all for territorial supremacy someday. Hell, they play their stupid games without a thought of making a patty melt of the human race. It all boils down to being reelected, I guess, to being in power. Bullets and votes. It seems like they go hand in hand.

# ORDER DIRECT